ALKALINE COOKBOOK

FOR BEGINNERS

Your Final 30-Day Alkaline Diet Meal Plan to Get your pH Back to Healthy in Less than a Week – Perfect for Beginners Who Do Not Have the Time and Skills to Make Effective Meals at Home

BY

Pierce Hum

Table of Contents

INTRODUCTION

Uses of alkaline diet

Verifiably, the clinical utilization of this diet has largely centered around forestalling repeat of kidney stones just as the counteraction of repetitive urinary parcel diseases, by depending on the perceived capacity of this diet to influence urinary pH. Quite a while back, this diet was utilized to change the sharpness of the urinary climate that the stones framed in, and could speculatively help keep stones from shaping or the advancement of UTIs. Notwithstanding, the insightful techniques that endeavored to figure the impacts of food on urinary pH were not exact besides in exceptionally broad terms, utilizing this diet troublesome. Thusly, drugs, which can all the more dependably adjust the pee pH, instead of diet change, have been the treatment of decision when attempting to modify pee pH.[15] While there have been ongoing upgrades in perceiving various factors that can influence corrosive discharge in the pee, the degree of detail expected to foresee the urinary pH dependent on diet is as yet overwhelming. Exact computations require exceptionally nitty gritty information on the healthful segments of each supper just as the pace of ingestion of supplements, which can shift significantly from one individual to another, making successful assessment of pee pH not presently feasible.

1. Apricot, almond & polenta cake

Prep:40 mins Cook:1 hr plus cooling Easy Serves 10

Ingredients:

- For the apricots
- 50g unsalted spread , in addition to extra for the tin
- 125g granulated sugar
- 8 new apricots , split and stoned (you may require more if the apricots are little)
- For the cake
- 150g unsalted spread , at room temperature, cubed

- 150g caster sugar
- 2 large eggs , daintily beaten
- 1 lemon , zested
- 1 tsp almond remove
- 50g plain flour
- 50g fine ground polenta
- 1½ tsp preparing powder
- 100g ground almonds
- 125ml milk
- 3 tbsp apricot jam , to coat
- crème fraîche or cream, to serve

Strategy:

1. Spread a 20-23cm round cake tin. On the off chance that it has a free base, you should wrap the outside with foil to keep any of the caramel from spilling. Heat the oven to 200C/180C fan/gas 6. For the apricots, put the granulated sugar and 75ml water into a pot. Heat gradually until the sugar has broken down. At the point when the sugar has softened, bring to the bubble and watch the syrup until it begins to go to a profound golden shading. Eliminate from the heat and add the spread.

Mix until it has liquefied. Fill the tin, at that point lay the apricots in it, cut-side down.

2. For the cake, beat together the margarine and sugar until light with an electric whisk. Add the egg a little at a time, then the zing and almond extricate. Combine every one of the dry ingredients as one, at that point overlap them steadily into the egg combination, exchanging with the milk. Spoon this absurd and heat for 50 mins. To test it's heated, drive a stick into the middle. It should tell the truth.

3. Leave the cake to cool for 15 mins, at that point run a blade in the middle of the cake and within the tin and modify it onto a plate. In the event that any of the apricot parts get abandoned in the tin cautiously scoop them up – attempting to keep their shape flawless and not squash them to an extreme – and set them back, cut-side up, on the cake. Leave the cake to cool, or serve warm in the event that you need.

4. Heat the apricot jam with 2 tbsp of water. When the jam has broken down, push it through a strainer to eliminate the pieces of apricot. Leave it to cool a little – else it

overcooks the apricots, which ought to be entirely cooked and not imploding – at that point paint the jam thickly on the highest point of the cake. Leave this to set a little, at that point present with crème fraîche or cream, on the off chance that you like.

2. Apricot, cardamom & pistachio ice lollies

Prep:20 mins plus 4 hrs freezing, no cook Easy

Makes 10 x 80ml lollies

Ingredients:

- 20 apricots (approx 750g), stripped, split and stoned
- 100g clear nectar
- 50g brilliant caster sugar
- 1 tsp ground cardamom
- 75g pistachios , finely chopped

Strategy:

1. Put the apricots in a blender and interaction until smooth. Pour the blend through a fine

cross section sifter, apportioning 500ml of purée. Add the nectar, sugar, 100ml water and the cardamom, and combine as one until smooth and uniformly consolidated.

2. Split the blend between the 10 depressions of your ice lolly form (see beneath for where to purchase). Put the shape in the cooler and chill for 30-45 mins or until simply beginning to freeze. Supplement the lolly sticks and leave to freeze for in any event 4 hrs or until frozen strong.

3. To eliminate the lollies, dunk the shape in steaming hot water for a couple of moments, at that point cautiously eliminate the lollies, plunging each into the chopped pistachios to serve.

Formula TIPS

Need TO MAKE A BIG BATCH?

1. In the event that you need to make in excess of 10 lollies however just have one shape, eliminate the lollies, wrap them exclusively in stick film and store them in a hermetically sealed holder in the cooler. They will keep for

as long as one month, however are best eaten inside about fourteen days.

2. COOL KIT
3. You can discover ice lolly forms and wooden candy sticks all things considered large grocery stores.

3. Apricot & ginger frangipane tart

Prep:30 mins Cook:50 mins plus chilling and cooling More effort Serves 6 – 8

Ingredients:

- For the baked good
- 200g plain flour
- 100g virus spread , cubed
- 50g brilliant caster sugar
- scarcely any drops vanilla concentrate
- 1 egg yolk
- For the frangipane
- 100g margarine , mollified
- 100g brilliant caster sugar
- 2 eggs
- 140g ground almond

- 75g plain flour , in addition to extra for tidying
- 2 balls stem ginger in syrup, finely chopped, in addition to 3 tbsp syrup
- 8-10 apricots , stoned and quartered
- To serve
- icing sugar, crème fraîche and vanilla bean paste (optional)

Technique:

1. To make the baked good, tip the flour, spread and a touch of salt into a food processor. Heartbeat until the blend looks like breadcrumbs. Add the sugar and heartbeat once more. Add the vanilla, egg and 1-2 tbsp super cold water, and heartbeat until the batter simply meets up. Tip out and shape into a plate. Carry out the cake on a softly floured surface and line a 22cm free lined tart tin, squeezing it into the sides. Chill for 30 mins.

2. In the interim, set up the frangipane. Using an electric whisk, beat the margarine until rich, at that point add the sugar and keep beating until light and feathery. Continuously add the eggs, beating great after every option, at that point

mix in the almonds, flour, ginger and 1 tbsp ginger syrup.

3. Heat oven to 180C/160C fan/gas 4 and put in a preparing plate to heat. Spoon the frangipane into the tart case and smooth. Stick the apricots into the frangipane. Move to the heating plate and prepare for 40-50 mins (cover with foil after 30 mins if the tart is taking on a lot tone) until the natural product is delicate and a stick jabbed in the frangipane confesses all.

4. Leave the tart to cool in the tin for 10 mins, at that point move to a wire rack. Heat the leftover ginger syrup in a skillet until thickened, and coat the tart with it. Serve warm or chilly, tidied with icing sugar, with a touch of crème fraîche blended in with a little vanilla bean paste, on the off chance that you like.

4.   Any-roast apricot & pecan stuffing

Prep:20 mins Cook:10 mins Easy Makes 4 batches

Ingredients:

- 50g spread
- 2 onions , split and cut
- 4 celery sticks, chopped
- 200g semi-dried apricot , split
- 3 garlic cloves , chopped
- 140g walnut , generally broken
- 1 tsp ground nutmeg
- 200g new breadcrumb
- 500g pack pork mince
- 1 large egg
- 3 tbsp chopped delicate thyme leaf

- little pack chopped parsley

Strategy:

1. Dissolve the spread in a large dish, add the onions and celery, and momentarily cook until they begin to mollify. Mix in the apricots and garlic, and cook a couple of mins more. Add the walnuts and nutmeg, and cook, blending until the nuts are delicately toasted. Leave to cool.

2. Mix in the breadcrumbs, mince, egg and spices with 1 tsp salt and heaps of pepper, at that point partition the blend into 4, gather into packs and freeze. Will save for a very long time.

3. One bunch will make 12 stuffing balls or can be utilized to stuff cook pork or chicken. Two clusters will fill a 1lb portion tin, fixed with smudgy bacon that can be cut, while 2 - 3 will stuff a medium-to-large turkey.

4. Cook at 200C/180C/gas 6 for 30 mins if folding into balls, 45 mins if cooking in a portion tin, or use to stuff the neck of your number one meal bird, cooking for a similar time as shown in the formula.

5. Golden couscous with apricots & crispy onions

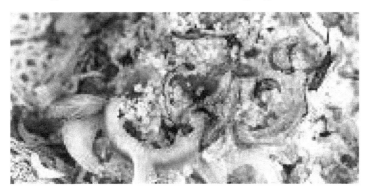

Prep:15 mins Cook:20 mins Easy Serves 6

Ingredients:

- 500g couscous
- 1 vegetable stock solid shape
- 2 tsp turmeric
- 1 tsp ground cinnamon
- 100g dried apricot , chopped
- 3 red onions , meagerly cut
- 1 tsp caster sugar
- about 500ml vegetable or sunflower oil
- zing and juice 1 lemon
- 2 tbsp olive oil
- little bundle coriander , chopped
- little modest bunch mint , chopped, a couple of leaves saved

Technique:

1. Heat up a pot. Tip the couscous into a large bowl, disintegrate in the stock shape, at that point add the turmeric, cinnamon and apricots, and season well. Pour over 500ml bubbling water, give everything a speedy mix, at that point cover with stick film and leave for 5 mins.

2. Put a large portion of the cut onions in a bowl with a decent spot of salt and the sugar, pour over sufficient bubbling water to cover and leave to soak for 10 mins. (This will eliminate a portion of the onions' causticity and turn them a wonderful radiant pink tone.)

3. Heat sufficient oil to come about 5cm up the side of a profound pan. Once hot, fry the excess onions in bunches for 1-2 mins until brilliant and firm. Channel on kitchen paper and sprinkle with salt.

4. Go through a fork to cushion the couscous. Channel the soaks onions and mix through the couscous with the lemon zing and juice, olive oil and spices. Tip onto a serving platter or bowl and disperse with the fresh onions and mint leaves.

6. Giant peach, nectarine & apricot meringue tart

Prep:20 mins Cook:35 mins More effort Serves 8

Ingredients:

- 30-33cm puff cake round sheet (we utilized Marie La Pâte Feuilletée), or roll your own from a 375g square
- 100g crème fraîche , in addition to extra to serve (optional)
- 1 large egg , in addition to 2 egg whites
- 100g ground almond
- 1 tsp vanilla concentrate
- 140g caster sugar

- 3-5 stone natural products (a combination of peaches, nectarines and apricots), cut
- 2 tbsp peach, apricot or nectarine jam
- ½ tsp almond extricate (optional)
- 1 tsp cornflour
- 25g toasted chipped almond

Strategy:

1. Heat oven to 200C/180C fan/gas 6. Lay the cake on a large preparing sheet and imprint a line 2cm from the edge with a blade. Heat for 10-12 mins until puffed up, brilliant and fresh under. Blend the crème fraîche, entire egg, ground almonds, vanilla concentrate and 40g of the sugar together.

2. Push the focal point of the cake down and spread this with the almond and crème fraîche blend, at that point top with the natural product. Warm the jam in the microwave, at that point sifter and brush everywhere on the organic product. Prepare in the oven for 10 mins.

3. In the mean time, whisk the egg whites until firm in a major blending bowl. Add the excess 100g sugar, the almond remove, if using, and

cornflour, and whisk again to a thick, smooth reflexive meringue. After 10 mins, eliminate the tart from the oven and go down to 160C/140C fan/gas 3. Touch the meringue in spoonfuls over the tart, at that point dissipate over the almonds. Heat for another 10-12 mins until the meringue feels fresh to contact. Eat at room temperature with more crème fraîche.

7. Apricot & marzipan twist

Cook:30 mins 45 mins + overnight soaking and rising More effort Serves 12

Ingredients:

- For the batter
- 250g solid white bread flour
- 50g unsalted spread , mollified
- 150ml entire milk
- 10g quick activity dried yeast
- 1 large egg , beaten
- For the filling
- 120g dried apricot , chopped
- 150ml squeezed orange
- 90g unsalted margarine
- 70g light muscovado sugar

- 35g plain flour
- 60g raisin
- 65g chopped pecan
- ground zing 1 orange
- 200g marzipan
- To wrap up
- 50g apricot jam
- 200g icing sugar , blended in with enough water to make a runny icing

Strategy:

1. The prior night, put apricots and squeezed orange in a bowl and put away.
2. To make the mixture, put flour, 1 tsp salt, spread, milk, yeast and egg in a bowl, and combine as one to frame a batter. Turn the batter out onto a gently floured surface and manipulate for 6 mins.
3. Move batter to a blending bowl. Cover, at that point put away to ascend in a warm spot for 1 hr.
4. In the interim, channel the apricots. In a blending bowl, cream the spread and muscovado sugar until soft. Blend in the apricots, flour, raisins, pecans and orange zing.

5. Turn the risen batter out onto a delicately floured surface. Carry it out to a square shape, around 25 x 33cm. Uniformly spread over the apricot blend, at that point carry out the marzipan and lay it on top. Move up the square shape firmly so it would appear that a Swiss roll. Roll marginally, at that point cut lengthways along the move, leaving 1 end joined. Contort 2 lengths together, at that point shape into a ring on a heating sheet fixed with preparing material. Put away to ascend for 1 hr.

6. Heat oven to 200C/180C fan/gas 6. Prepare the curve for 30 mins until risen and dull brilliant. Towards the finish of the heating time, tenderly warm the apricot jam in a little container. Brush the newly prepared portion with the warm jam to coat it, at that point put it to the side to cool. Once cooled, sprinkle the curve intensely with the runny icing.

8.   Spiced apricot chutney

Prep:20 mins Cook:40 mins - 45 mins Easy

Makes 2kg

Ingredients:

- 1kg apricot
- 2 red onions
- 5cm piece ginger
- 2 apples
- 2 red chillies
- 1 tsp Chinese five-flavor powder
- 1 tsp paprika
- 1 tsp coarsely squashed dark peppercorn
- 1 tsp salt
- 400ml juice vinegar
- 450g granulated sugar

Strategy:

1. Split and stone the apricots, at that point hack them into little pieces. Strip and coarsely slash the onions, ginger and apples, and put in a food processor. Generally slash the chillies and add to the food processor alongside the seeds. Barrage until finely chopped, at that point tip into a large skillet and add the flavors, salt and vinegar. Bring to the bubble, at that point turn down and stew for 10 mins, blending incidentally.

2. Add the apricots and get back to the bubble. Stew for a further 10 mins until the apricots are beginning to mellow, at that point tip in the sugar and mix until disintegrated. Increment the heat and bubble for 15-20 mins, blending periodically, until the combination is thick and leaves a concise path when a wooden spoon is hauled across the foundation of the dish.

3. Pot into warm clean containers and mark. Store for as long as a year in a cool dry spot.

9.   Apricot conserve

Prep:20 mins Cook:35 mins More effort 3 x 500g jars

Ingredients:

- 1 ½kg apricot
- 200ml squeezed apple
- 1kg saving sugar
- juice 1 large lemon
- handle of margarine

Technique:

1. Several little plates in the cooler. Divide and stone the apricots, cleave the tissue, at that point put in a large skillet with the squeezed apple. Pop open a portion of the pieces to remove the nut inside (this is not difficult to do on the off chance that you open with the level side of a weighty pan), add them to the skillet

– this is optional, yet gives additional flavor. Bring to the bubble, lessen the heat and stew for 10 mins, until the apricots are softened.

2. Mix in the sugar and lemon juice, at that point mix above and beyond a moderate heat to break down the sugar. Increment the heat and bubble for around 20 mins until jam has set. Test by spooning a little jam onto one of your virus plates. After a second push the jam with your finger; if the jam wrinkles, it is prepared. On the off chance that not, get back to the bubble for a further 5 mins, test once more.

3. Eliminate from the heat, skim off any rubbish, at that point mix in the spread to break down any leftover filth. Cool for 10 mins, mix once more, at that point spoon into warm disinfected containers. Seal, name, at that point store in the cooler for 4 a month and a half.

Formula TIPS

Saving YOUR CONSERVE FOR LONGER

1. This save is low in sugar so it should be kept in the ice chest, except if you 'bottle' it whenever

it is jolted. To do this, set the containers in a large, profound skillet fixed with a tea towel, ensuring the tops are safely on. Weave another tea towel around the containers to stop them thumping together. Pour over water to cover the containers totally, at that point bring to the bubble. Stew for 60 minutes, at that point leave in the water to cool. The jam would now be able to be kept in a cool, dim spot for as long as a year.

10. Guinea fowl tagine with chickpeas, squash & apricots

Prep:20 mins Cook:1 hr and 20 mins More effort Serves 6

Ingredients:

- 3 tbsp olive oil
- 2 guinea fowl , jointed like a chicken (request that your butcher do this or see our video on the most proficient method to joint a chicken, in 'Attempt', beneath)
- 2 onions , generally chopped
- 2 garlic cloves , chopped
- 1 butternut squash or little pumpkin, stripped, deseeded and cut into large lumps
- 1 tbsp ras-el-hanout
- 1 tsp ground cumin

- 1 tsp ground coriander
- ¼ tsp ground ginger
- 1 large cinnamon stick
- little crush of clear nectar
- large spot of saffron , absorbed 1 tbsp bubbling water
- juice 1 lemon
- 850ml chicken stock
- 400g can chickpea , depleted and flushed
- 200g dried apricot
- little bundle coriander
- couscous or rice, to serve

Technique:

2. Heat the oil in a large, shallow flameproof goulash dish. Season the guinea fowl pieces and brown them – in clumps, in the event that important – eliminate to a plate.

3. Fry the onions in a similar dish until softened, at that point add the garlic and squash, cooking for 1-2 mins. Tip in the flavors and cook for a couple of mins prior to adding the nectar, saffron and lemon juice. Pour in the chicken stock and the chickpeas.

4. Lower the guinea fowl pieces in the stock and add the apricots. Cover the dish and stew everything delicately for 50 mins-1 hr, until the fowl and squash are both delicate. Mix through the coriander and present with couscous or rice.

11. Apricot & almond Chelsea buns

Prep:30 mins Cook:22 mins Plus rising and proving More effort Makes 8

Ingredients:

- For the mixture
- 450g solid white flour , in addition to extra for cleaning
- 2 x 7g sachets simple mix yeast
- 50g caster sugar
- 150ml warm milk
- 1 egg , beaten
- 50g unsalted margarine , dissolved, in addition to extra for lubing
- oil , for lubing
- For the garnish

- 25g softened margarine , in addition to extra for lubing
- 85g dried apricot , finely chopped
- 85g toasted chipped almond , in addition to a couple of extra to improve
- 25g caster sugar
- 2 tbsp apricot jam

Technique:

1. Put the flour, yeast, caster sugar and 1 tsp salt into a large blending bowl and blend well. Make a well in the middle and pour in the warm milk, 50ml warm water, the beaten egg and the softened spread. Combine everything as one to frame a batter – start with a wooden spoon and get done with your hands. In the event that the mixture is excessively dry, add somewhat more warm water; if it's excessively wet, add more flour.

2. Massage in the bowl or on a floured surface until the mixture gets smooth and springy. Move to a clean, gently lubed bowl and cover freely with a spotless, sodden tea towel. Leave in a warm spot to ascend until generally

multiplied in size – this will take around 1 hr relying upon how warm the room is.

3. Heat oven to 200C/180C fan/gas 6 and oil a profound 21 or 23cm cake tin. Tip the risen mixture out onto a softly floured surface and work for a couple of secs. Carry out the batter to an unpleasant 20 x 30cm square shape. Spread the margarine equally ridiculous, at that point sprinkle with the chopped apricots, almonds and sugar. Move up immovably like a Swiss move from one of the long sides – hosing the open edge to help it stick on the off chance that you need to. Cut into 8 even cuts with a sharp blade, shape into 8 round pinwheels, at that point organize in the tin, cut-side up. Cover with a perfect, soggy tea towel and demonstrate in a warm spot for around 20 mins until generally multiplied in size.

4. Heat the buns for 10 mins, at that point lower oven to 180C/160C fan/gas 4. Cook for 10 mins more until brilliant brown. Liquefy the jam with 1 tbsp water, brush everywhere on the buns, at that point sprinkle with a couple of more chipped almonds.

Formula TIPS

MORE EASTER BAKING

1. Whenever you've dominated this mixture, use it as the reason for Hot cross buns and Spiced natural product portion.

12. Dried apricot jam

Prep:5 mins Cook:1 hr Plus overnight soaking

More effort Makes 4 x 300g jars

Ingredients:

- 500g entire dried apricot , chopped
- juice 3 large lemons
- 1 ½kg jam sugar

Strategy:

1. Put the apricots in a large dish, add 1.5 liters water, cover and leave for the time being to splash.

2. Following day, place a little plate in the ice chest to chill. Put the apricots and water on the hob, at that point add the lemon squeeze and bring to the bubble. Decrease the heat, at that

point stew for 30 mins or until the apricots are delicate and beginning to separate.

3. Eliminate from the heat and add the sugar, mixing until it breaks up. Get back to the heat and bubble quickly for 20 mins or until setting point is reached. To check this, eliminate the plate from the refrigerator, put a spoonful of jam onto the plate and pop it back in the cooler for a couple of mins – the jam should wrinkle when you push it with your finger. A sugar thermometer will likewise give you the setting point of jam, which is 105C.

4. Cautiously empty the jam into hot cleaned containers, top with a plate of wax paper or heating material, seal with a cover, at that point leave to cool and set. The jam will keep going for a half year unopened in a cool, dim pantry.

13. Apricot & raspberry tart

Prep:15 mins Cook:25 mins Easy Serves 4

Ingredients:

- 3 large sheets filo cake (or 6 little)
- 2 tbsp margarine , dissolved
- 3 tbsp apricot moderate
- 6 ready apricots , stoned and generally cut
- 85g raspberries
- 2 tsp caster sugar

Strategy:

1. Let the filo come to room temperature for around 10 mins before use. Put a preparing plate into the oven and heat oven to 200C/180C fan/gas 6.

2. Brush every large sheet of filo with liquefied margarine, layer on top of one another, at that point overlap fifty-fifty so you have a more modest square shape 6 layers thick. On the off chance that using little sheets simply stack on top of one another. Overlap in the edges of the baked good base to make a 2cm boundary, at that point spread the apricot save inside the line. Cautiously slide the cake base on to the hot heating plate and prepare for 5 mins.

3. Eliminate from oven, organize apricots over the tart and brush with any extra dissolved spread. Prepare for another 10 mins, at that point dissipate on raspberries and sprinkle with sugar. Prepare for a last 10 mins until the cake is brilliant brown and fresh.

14. Quinoa & apricot muffins

Prep:10 mins Cook:20 mins Easy Makes 12

Ingredients:

- 50g quinoa
- 100g finely chopped dried apricot
- 250g tub quark
- 3 large eggs
- 1 tsp vanilla concentrate
- 2 tbsp rapeseed oil
- 2 little ground apples (no compelling reason to strip)
- zing and juice 1 little orange
- 50g pumpkin seed , in addition to somewhat extra

- 50g wholemeal plain flour
- 50g ground almond
- 2 tbsp chia seeds
- 25g wheatgerm
- 1 ½ tsp heating powder

Technique:

1. Heat oven to 180C/160C fan/gas 4 and line a 12-opening biscuit tin with paper cases. Tip the quinoa and apricots into a little container with 300ml water, bring to the bubble, at that point turn the heat directly down, cover and stew for 20 mins until the water has been consumed and the quinoa is cooked. Check oftentimes that it doesn't bubble dry.

2. Then, beat the quark with the eggs, remove, oil, apples, and orange zing and juice. Mix in the cooled quinoa blend, at that point crease in the pumpkin seeds, flour, ground almonds, chia seeds, wheatgerm and heating powder. Spoon into the biscuit cases, disperse with a couple of pumpkin seeds and prepare for 20 mins.

15. Fragrant shepherd's pie with apricots

Prep:3 hrs and 50 mins Easy Serves 8

Ingredients:

- 1kg minced sheep
- 2 onions , generally chopped
- finger length piece new root ginger
- 2 garlic cloves , generally chopped
- 1 tbsp cumin
- 2 tbsp cinnamon
- ½ tsp hot stew powder
- 1 tbsp olive oil
- 6 large tomatoes , generally chopped
- 2 tbsp tomato purée
- 1 tbsp nectar
- 550ml sheep or meat stock

- 200g dried apricot , chopped
- large pack coriander , leaves just, generally chopped
- For the crush
- 1 ¼kg yams , stripped and cut into pieces
- 1 ¼kg potatoes , stripped and cut into large pieces
- 50g spread
- sprinkle of milk
- toasted cumin seeds , to serve

Strategy:

1. Brown the sheep in groups in a large, profound griddle (there's no compelling reason to add oil). When each clump is browned, move it to a sifter and pour off the overabundance fat from the container prior to cooking the following group. Put away the browned mince and crash the dish with some kitchen paper. Whizz the onions, ginger, garlic and flavors together in a food processor until finely chopped and somewhat thick (you can add a drop of water in the event that you need to), tip into a similar dish with the oil. Cook over a medium

heat for 5-6 mins until the onion is softened and the flavors become fragrant.

2. Return the meat to the skillet alongside the chopped tomatoes and purée, nectar and the stock. Bring to the bubble, cover and stew for 1 hr, adding the apricots after 30 mins. The sheep and apricots ought to be delicate, and the sauce thickened; if it's somewhat wet actually, stew, revealed, for another 10 mins. Eliminate from the heat, mix in the coriander leaves and season well.

3. While the sheep is cooking, set up the potato besting. Heat up the potatoes in salted water for 15 mins until delicate. Once cooked, channel well and squash with the margarine, preparing and enough milk to give you a rich consistency.

4. Heat oven to 200C/fan 180C/gas 6. Tip the sheep blend into a large ovenproof dish and heap the crush generally finished. (It helps on the off chance that you start from the edges and work your way towards the center.) If you're making ahead, cool at that point freeze the pie now, uncovered. Once frozen, cover

with stick film and use inside multi month, thawing out completely prior to reheating.

5. Heat for 40 mins from warm, or for 1 hr from cold, until the fixing is starting to brown and the filling is hot. In the event that you like, dissipate with some toasted cumin seeds to serve.

16. Apricot crumb squares

Prep:20 mins - 25 mins Cook:45 mins - 50 minsEasy Serves 16

Ingredients:

- For the garnish
- 175g plain flour
- 140g light muscovado sugar
- 140g margarine , softened
- 1 tsp ground cinnamon
- For the cake
- 175g margarine , softened
- 200g brilliant caster sugar
- 3 large eggs
- 175g plain flour
- 1 tsp heating powder
- 2-3 tbsp milk

- 8 new apricots , quartered (or canned in regular juice)
- icing sugar for cleaning

Technique:

1. Preheat oven to fan 160C/ordinary 180C/gas 4 and margarine a shallow 22cm square cake tin. Put every one of the garnish ingredients in a food processor with 1/2 tsp salt and mix to make a tacky disintegrate.

2. Using an electric hand whisk or wooden spoon, mix the cake ingredients, with the exception of milk and apricots, slowly adding sufficient milk to make a velvety blend that drops from the spoon. Spread in the tin and disperse with apricots. Top with the disintegrate and press down.

3. Heat for 45-50 minutes until brilliant and a stick confesses all. Cool in tin, cut into 16 squares and residue with icing sugar. (Keeps as long as 5 days in a plastic compartment in the ice chest.)

17. Apricot French toast

Prep:10 mins Cook:15 mins Easy Serves 4

Ingredients:

- 50g spread
- 6 apricots , split and stoned
- 200g/8oz caramel sauce (we utilized Bonne Maman confiture de caramel)
- 350g instant vanilla custard
- 8 little, thick cuts brioche or white bread, or 4 large cuts, cut slantingly

Strategy:

1. Dissolve 1 tbsp spread in a medium-size skillet. Put in the apricots, cut-side down, and delicately fry for 2-3 mins. Flip over and cook for 1 min more until daintily brilliant. Add the

caramel to the container and liquefy until sassy – if it's still too thick to even think about covering the natural product, add a sprinkle of water. Keep warm.

2. Blend the custard in with 4 tbsp of water to release, at that point dunk in the bread cuts, going to cover altogether. Liquefy a large portion of the excess spread in a large non-stick skillet. Softly shake off any abundance custard combination from a large portion of the bread cuts and fry in the margarine for 2 mins each side until brilliant. Rehash with outstanding spread and bread, at that point serve hot with the caramel apricots.

18. Crunchy oat clusters with peach

Prep:5 mins Cook:15 mins - 20 mins Easy

Serves 6

Ingredients:

- 50g (around 7) delicate prepared to-eat dried apricots (we utilized Crazy Jack natural, since they are sans sulfur)
- ½ tbsp rapeseed oil
- 3 large eggs , whites just (see tip to go through the yolks)
- 200g porridge oats
- 1 tbsp cinnamon
- 1 tbsp vanilla concentrate
- 25g parched coconut
- 25g chipped almonds
- 25g pumpkin seeds

- 3 x 120g pots bio yogurt
- 3 peaches , to serve

Technique:

1. Heat oven to 180C/160C fan/gas 4 and line a large preparing plate with heating material.

2. Tip the apricots, oil and egg whites into a bowl (see tip box for how to go through the egg yolks), at that point barrage with a hand blender until smooth. Mix in the oats, cinnamon and vanilla, at that point overlap through the dried up coconut, almonds and pumpkin seeds.

3. Squeeze groups of the blend together to make surface in the granola, at that point disperse over the lined preparing plate in a solitary layer. Prepare for 15 mins, at that point throw (turning the larger parts) and heat for a further 10 mins until brilliant and crunchy.

4. Cool the granola totally on the plate, at that point pack into a large impermeable container or compartment. In case you're following our Healthy Diet Plan, serve two segments more than three days, filling the foundation of each

bowl with yogurt (½ pot for each part) and garnish with a large portion of a peach, cut.

Formula TIPS

Join TO OUR HEALTHY DIET PLAN

1. This formula is essential for our free Healthy Diet Plan. Join today and we'll send you seven days of triple-tried, healthfully enhanced recipes, in addition to master tips to help you look and feel your absolute best!
2. Go through THE EGG YOLKS
3. Try not to discard the egg yolks – freeze them for one more day. You can utilize them in fried eggs, omelets and to improve pureed potatoes when you're not after the Healthy Diet Plan.

19. Panna cotta with apricot compote

Prep:20 mins Cook:20 mins Plus setting More effort Serves 4

Ingredients:

- 3 level tsp gelatine (or veggie gelatine or agar)
- 500ml soya milk (we utilized So Good)
- zing 1 lemon
- 1 vanilla case , split
- sprinkle of rum liquor
- 50g brilliant caster sugar
- For the compote
- 350g ready apricot
- 50g caster sugar

Technique:

1. Sprinkle the gelatine onto 3 tbsp water and drench for 5 mins. Scratch the seeds out of the vanilla case into the container and put the case into the milk. Put the soya milk, zing, vanilla unit, sugar and rum into a dish. Heat until the fluid simply goes to the bubble (if using veggie gelatine, you'll need to carry it to the bubble – check pack guidelines), at that point eliminate from the heat and mix in the gelatine. Cool for 10 mins. In the event that the gelatine clusters together, whisk altogether. Strain the milk blend, at that point split between 4 ramekins. Cover and refrigerate until set (roughly 2 hrs).

2. Divide and stone the apricots. Put the sugar and 150ml water into a dish, at that point heat until the sugar has broken up. Add the apricots and cook over a delicate heat for 12-15 mins or until the apricots are delicate, at that point leave to cool. Serve in a dish close by the panna cotta.

Formula TIPS

MAKE IT VEGAN

1. On the off chance that you are cooking for a veggie lover or vegetarian, substitute the gelatine for agar (accessible from wellbeing food shops). It works distinctively to gelatine – you don't have to cool the custard to get it to set; you simply splash it, at that point add it to the custard soon after it's made.

20. Apricot & hazelnut mince pies

Prep:30 mins Cook:20 mins - 25 mins Plus chilling Easy Serves 10 – 12

Ingredients:

- For the cake
- 170g without gluten flour
- ½ tsp cinnamon
- 100g unsalted spread
- 1 tbsp caster sugar
- For the mincemeat
- 140g semi-dried apricot , finely diced
- 85g semi-dried fig , finely diced
- 100g pack toasted hazelnut
- 1 tsp each ground cinnamon , ground nutmeg and blended flavor

- ground zing and juice of 1 orange
- 50g spread
- 1 banana , chopped
- 3 tbsp cognac
- icing sugar , to serve

Strategy:

1. To make the baked good: put the flour and cinnamon into the bowl of a food processor. Add the spread and heartbeat until it would seem that fine breadcrumbs. Sprinkle in the sugar and 3 tbsp cold water, and heartbeat until the combination begins to bunch together, around 30 secs. Tip the combination onto a board and delicately press the baked good until it meets up into a ball – add water in the event that it feels dry. Enclose the cake by stick film and chill for 30 mins.

2. Heat oven to 190C/fan 170C/gas 5. Roll the cake on a softly floured surface to the thickness of £1 coin. Using a 7cm shaper, cut out 10-12 circles and use to fix a 12-opening bun tin with them. Utilize a 6cm shaper for the tops, or utilize a 6cm star shaper to make star shapes. Chill both.

3. Make the mincemeat: put every one of the ingredients into a food processor and heartbeat on and off until equally chopped. Spoon 1-2 tsp into every tart, hose the edge of the cake base with water and sit a more modest baked good plate or star on top. Using scissors, clip an opening in the cover, on the off chance that you've made round tops. Heat for 12-15 mins until brilliant brown. Lift onto a wire rack to cool and dig with icing sugar.

21. Chickpea tagine soup

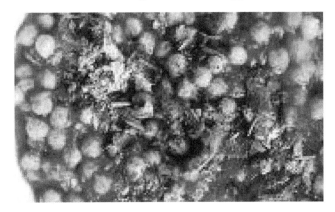

Prep:10 mins Cook:30 mins Easy Serves 4

Ingredients:

- 2 red peppers
- 1 tbsp rapeseed oil
- 1 red onion , daintily cut
- 2 large garlic cloves , squashed
- 2 tsp ground coriander
- 1 tsp ground cumin
- 2 tbsp rose harissa paste
- 2 x 400g jars chickpeas , depleted and washed
- 1 ½l low-salt veg stock
- 150g kale , chopped
- 1 lemon , zested and squeezed
- 50g dried apricots , finely chopped
- 1/2 little bundle parsley , finely chopped

- without fat common yogurt , to serve (optional)

Strategy:

1. Heat the flame broil to its most elevated setting. Divide and deseed the peppers, at that point lay cut-side down on a preparing sheet fixed with foil. Flame broil for 10-15 mins, or until rankled and softened. Leave until adequately cool to deal with, at that point eliminate and dispose of the skins. Cut the simmered peppers into meager strips.

2. Heat the oil in a large pot over a low heat. Fry the onion for 8-10 mins until softened. Mix through the garlic, coriander, cumin and harissa paste and cook for 1 min more. Add the chickpeas and stock, bring to the bubble and stew for 15 mins, covered.

3. Mix the peppers through the soup with the kale, lemon zing and juice, and apricots and cook, covered, for another 5 mins. Scoop the soup into bowls and present with the chopped parsley dissipated over and a spot of yogurt, on the off chance that you like.

Works out in a good way For

Herby broccoli and pea soup

Curried spinach and lentil soup

Smooth chilled basil, pea and lettuce soup

22. Apricot & pistachio pavlova

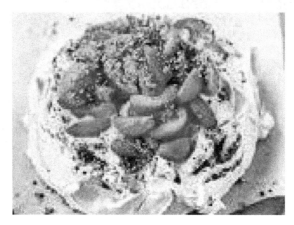

Total time2 hrs Takes 1¾ - 2 hours, plus cooling More effort Serves 6

Ingredients:

- 2 tsp cornflour
- 2 tsp vanilla concentrate
- 2 tsp white wine vinegar , or some other wine or juice vinegar
- 5 large egg whites
- 300g brilliant caster sugar
- 50g shelled pistachio , generally chopped
- 650g ready new apricots
- 3 tbsp Cointreau or other orange enhanced liquer
- 4 tbsp icing sugar , or much more to taste

- 568ml container whipping cream or twofold cream

Technique:

1. Preheat the oven to 140C/gas 1/fan 120C and line a heating sheet with non-stick material paper. In a little bowl, mix the cornflour, vanilla concentrate and vinegar to a smooth paste.

2. Whisk the egg whites until hardened in a different clean bowl. Slowly race in the sugar a little at a time to make a thick and shiny meringue, at that point rush in the cornflour paste until well combined.Spoon the blend on to the paper, at that point spread, without straightening it, to frame a 23cm/9in round. Whirl the edges with the rear of the spoon to give stunning delicate creases and pinnacles. Dissipate a large portion of the pistachios over the meringue and heat for 60 minutes, by which time it will feel fresh on the off chance that you tap it. Mood killer the oven and leave the pavlova to cool with the oven entryway open.

3. Put away 450g/1lb of the apricots and generally cleave the rest, disposing of the stones. Purée the chopped apricots, at that point push them through a sifter with a metal spoon. Mix in the alcohol and improve with 3 tbsp of the icing sugar, or enough to improve as you like it.

4. Delicately whip the cream so it's delicate and surging, at that point spoon over the pavlova. Cut the held 450g/1lb apricots down the middle, dispose of the stones, at that point cut into wedges. Disperse them over the whipped cream alongside the excess pistachios. Residue with the remainder of the icing sugar and present with the apricot purée.

23. Apricot & almond bistro tart

Total time40 mins Takes 30-40 minutes Easy Serves 8

Ingredients:

- 370g pack prepared moved puff cake
- 50g ground almond
- 900g ready new apricots , split and stoned
- 2 tbsp icing sugar
- maple syrup and cream , to serve (optional)

Strategy:

1. Preheat the oven to 220C/gas 7/fan 200C. Unroll the cake on to a daintily hosed heating sheet (this makes steam which assists puff with increasing the cake), at that point sprinkle

over the ground almonds. Lay the apricot parts over the top, nestling them intently together, straight up to the edge of the baked good.

2. Residue with the icing sugar and heat for 20-25 minutes until the sugar begins to caramelize a bit. On the off chance that you like, shower with maple syrup and serve hot, warm or cold. In the event that you truly need to enjoy, present with a spoonful of coagulated cream or a pouring of single cream.

24. Apricot & orange rice pudding

Prep:5 mins Cook:12 mins Easy Serves 4

Ingredients:

- 200g pudding rice
- 600ml skimmed milk
- enormous squeeze ground nutmeg
- 1 tbsp clear nectar , in addition to extra to serve
- 140g prepared to-eat dried apricot , generally chopped
- zing and juice 1 orange
- 4 tbsp diminished fat fromage frais
- modest bunch toasted cut almonds

Technique:

1. Put the rice, milk and nutmeg into a large microwaveable bowl. Cover with stick film, penetrate it, at that point cook on High for 5 mins. Mix and leave to represent 1 min, at that point get back to the microwave for a further 5-6 mins or until the rice is cooked and all the milk ingested. Eliminate from the microwave and represent a further 2 mins.

2. another microwaveable bowl and cook on High for 1 min until the apricots have plumped up. Mix the sweet apricots, fromage frais and a spot of orange zing into the rice. Serve straight away in bowls, finished off with a sprinkling of almonds, somewhat more orange zing and a shower of nectar to taste.

Formula TIPS

MAKING IT EXTRA CRUNCHY

1. Mix through 1 tbsp each toasted sesame seeds, pine nuts and pumpkin seeds toward the finish of cooking to make it extra crunchy.

2. MAKING IT FULL OF Fiber

3. Add an extra 50g chopped prunes, dates, dried figs or cranberries alongside the dried apricots.

25. Apricot gâteau Pithiviers

Prep:30 mins Cook:30 mins - 35 mins Plus chilling More effort Serves 10

Ingredients:

- For the filling
- 100g margarine , softened
- 140g brilliant caster sugar
- 1 egg yolk
- 100g ground almonds
- 1 tbsp plain flour
- 1 tbsp Grand Marnier or Disaronno
- 200g ready apricots , stoned and thickly cut
- For the cake case
- 500g pack of instant puff cake (or 2x 375g packs prepared moved Dorset cake)

- 1 egg , beaten
- 3 tbsp apricot jam

Strategy:

1. Beat the spread and sugar in a large bowl, at that point beat in the egg and egg yolk. Mix in the almonds, flour and alcohol, and blend well to a spreadable paste.

2. Carry out a large portion of the baked good and, using a sharp blade, cut out a circle roughly 25cm in distance across (utilize a supper plate as a guide). It ought to be about the thickness of 2 x £1 coins. Carry out the leftover cake and cut out another circle, somewhat larger than the first. In case you're using prepared moved baked good, cut a circle from each sheet and freeze what's left.

3. Spot the more modest circle on a heating plate and top with a large portion of the almond filling, leaving a 2.5cm boundary round the edge. Spread the apricots over, at that point put the remainder of the filling on top. Brush the line with beaten egg and set the excess cake circle on top, squeezing the edges solidly together.

4. With the rear of a blade, score lines round the external edge of the cake. Presently press the rear of the blade 1cm into the baked good edge at customary spans to give a scalloped appearance. Brush the top with more beaten egg and score bended lines transmitting from the focal point of the circle. Take care not to slice through the cake. Chill for 20 mins. The tart can be made ahead and frozen now or kept in the cooler for 2 days.

5. Heat oven to 200C/fan 180C/gas 6. Prepare for 30-35 mins until puffed and brilliant. Leave to cool on a preparing plate. To coat, dissolve the jam in a little dish and pass through a strainer. At that point brush over the baked good.

26. Spiced honey-glazed halloumi & fig salad

Prep:20 mins Cook:10 mins Easy Serves 8 as a starter or 20 canapés

Ingredients:

- 10 new figs , split
- 60g nectar
- 2 tsp ras el hanout
- 100ml olive oil
- 2 x 250g squares halloumi , thickly cut, at that point split
- 2 tbsp sherry vinegar
- 150g rocket
- 2 x 80g packs prosciutto
- 2 tbsp chipped almonds , toasted

Strategy:

1. Heat the barbecue to its most elevated setting. Put the fig parts on one portion of a heating sheet and sprinkle with a large portion of the nectar. Dry-fry the ras el hanout in a hot prospect min. Blend the leftover nectar in with the toasted ras el hanout and 2 tbsp of the olive oil. Throw the cuts of halloumi in the blend and spread out on the other portion of the preparing sheet. Flame broil everything for 3 mins, flip the halloumi over and set back under the barbecue for a further 3 mins or until the halloumi is brilliant and the figs are softened.
2. Whisk the leftover oil with the sherry vinegar and season to taste. Mastermind modest bunches of the rocket on six plates and sprinkle with the dressing. Top with the figs, halloumi and prosciutto, at that point get done with the toasted almonds.

Formula TIPS

Fill in AS CANAPéS
1. Slash the barbecued halloumi into 3cm pieces and cut the figs down the middle once more. Fold portions of prosciutto over a piece of halloumi and fig, at that point shower with somewhat nectar.

27. Fig sponge pudding

Prep:20 mins Cook:1 hr plus cooling Easy
Serves 6-8

Ingredients:
- 250g butter , softened, plus extra for the dish
- 5 tbsp golden syrup
- 4 tbsp honey
- 8 fresh figs
- 4 large eggs
- 250g golden caster sugar
- 250g self-raising flour
- 1 tsp baking powder
- 1 tsp vanilla extract
- For the topping
- 4 tbsp full-fat Greek yogurt
- 2-3 thyme sprigs (optional)
- extra virgin olive oil or honey, for drizzling (optional)

Method:
1. Heat the oven to 180C/160C fan/gas 4. Butter a 20 x 22cm ovenproof dish, then pour in the golden syrup and honey. Trim the stalks from the figs, then cut a deep cross·in the top, just

so they open out a bit, but be careful not to cut all the way through. Sit the figs upright on top of the syrup and put them in the oven to bake for 15-20 mins until softened and starting to caramelise a little at the edges.

2. While the figs are cooking, make the sponge mixture. Put the eggs, sugar, flour, baking powder, vanilla and butter in a bowl and use an electric whisk to beat until smooth.

3. Remove the dish from the oven, scoop the figs out with a slotted spoon and set aside. Once the syrup mixture has cooled in the dish, take spoonfuls of the sponge batter and gently place them on top of the syrup. It's best to do this all the way around the edge first, then end in the middle – this helps keep the syrup mixture separate. Smooth the batter out very gently to cover any gaps and seal the syrup mixture in.

4. Bake for 35-40 mins or until the sponge springs back when pressed. Allow to cool for around 5 mins or until just warm, then seconds before serving, dot the surface with eight small dollops of the yogurt. Top each mound with a baked fig, then scatter over some thyme leaves and drizzle with extra virgin olive oil, if you like.

RECIPE TIPS
FOR EXTRA CRUNCH
1. The crisp top of the pudding provides a great contrast of textures with the sponge centre, but if you want even more crunch, try crumbling over a couple of sesame brittle bars.

2. GOES WELL WITH
3. Coconut, rum & raisin rice pudding
4. Stuffed pasta bake bolognese
5. Slow-cooked pork, cider & sage hotpot

28. Rye pizza with figs, fennel, gorgonzola & hazelnuts

Prep:1 hr Cook:45 mins plus 2-3 hrs rising More effort makes 2 x 30cm pizzas

Ingredients:

- For the mixture
- 5g dynamic dried yeast
- 250g solid white flour
- 125g '00' flour
- 125g rye flour
- ½ tsp sugar
- 1 tsp olive oil
- semolina flour , for tidying
- For the garnish
- 1 large fennel bulb , any fronds saved
- juice 1/2 little lemon
- 1 tbsp olive oil
- 2 medium onions , split and finely cut
- ¼ tsp fennel seeds , coarsely squashed in a mortar
- some additional virgin olive oil , for showering
- 12 little figs , divided
- 1 ½ tbsp balsamic vinegar

- a little caster sugar , for sprinkling
- 180g gorgonzola (or veggie lover elective), broken into lumps
- 2 tbsp hazelnuts , split and toasted

Strategy:

1. To make the mixture, blend the yeast in a little bowl with 2 tbsp warm water and 1 tbsp solid white flour. Leave some place warm to 'wipe' for 20 mins or thereabouts (this disintegrates and initiates the yeast). Tip the three flours into a large bowl and make a well in the middle. Pour in the wiped yeast, 1 tsp salt, sugar, oil and 290ml warm water, and blend to shape a wet mixture. Manipulate for 10 mins until silky and flexible, at that point put in a spotless bowl, cover with a material and leave to twofold in size for 2 1/2 - 3 hrs.
2. Quarter the fennel bulb lengthways and eliminate any intense external leaves. Trim the foundation of each, meagerly cut with a blade or mandolin, at that point put in a bowl with the lemon squeeze so it doesn't become brown.
3. Heat the oil in a skillet, add the onions and a spot of salt, and fry over a medium heat for 7 mins. Add 1-2 tbsp of water, season with pepper, cover and cook on a low heat for 10 mins until softened. Add the majority of the fennel, alongside the fennel seeds and preparing, and cook for 3 mins, mixing now and then. In the event that the blend is as yet wet, reveal and bubble off any fluid.

4. An hour prior to cooking, heat the oven to its most noteworthy setting and put a preparing sheet or pizza stone in to heat. Tip the batter onto a softly floured surface, ply it somewhat, at that point split and fold each piece into a circle or harsh square. Lift the mixture and, while turning, stretch with your fingertips until each piece is 30-32cm across and as slender as conceivable with a marginally thicker edge.
5. Sprinkle two large preparing sheets with semolina and put the pizza bases on them. Top each base with the cooked onion and fennel blend, at that point the bits of crude fennel, leaving a 3cm line. Sprinkle with a little olive oil. Put the divided figs on top and spoon on a little balsamic vinegar and a sprinkle of sugar. Granulate over some pepper. Cautiously slide the principal pizza onto the heated preparing sheet in the oven. Heat for 8-12 mins until the mixture is brilliant and the figs caramelized. Partially through the cooking time, spot the pizza with the cheddar. Disperse on the toasted hazelnuts and any saved fennel fronds. Rehash with the subsequent pizza.

29. Fig, raspberry & cardamom pie

Prep:50 mins Cook:25 mins - 45 mins plus chilling, cook time depends on the size of your pie

Ingredients:
- For the baked good
- 225g cold unsalted margarine , chopped into little pieces
- 350g plain flour
- 50g icing sugar
- 1 large egg yolk (save the white for brushing the cake)
- For the filling
- 10-12 large figs , quartered
- 400g raspberries
- 50g brilliant caster sugar , in addition to extra for sprinkling
- 1 tbsp cornflour
- 8 cardamom cases
- ¼ tsp rosewater
- 1 tbsp fine polenta or ground almonds

- egg white , for brushing (held from making the cake)
- cream , crème fraîche, regular yogurt or soured cream, to serve

Technique:
- First make the cake. Put the margarine and flour in a food processor with 1/4 tsp salt and mix until the combination looks like soggy breadcrumbs. Or then again do this by scouring the spread and flour together in a major bowl with your fingertips. Add the sugar and momentarily whizz again or mix to join.
- Whisk the egg yolk with 2 tbsp cold water, and sprinkle over the flour blend. Utilize the beat catch to mix the blend again, continue to go until it begins to shape larger bunches. In the event that the blend appears to be excessively dry, add somewhat more water a tsp or 2 all at once, yet close to 3 tsp altogether.
- Tip out onto a work surface and momentarily ply the batter to unite it into a smooth ball. Abstain from workaholic behavior or it will get extreme. Straighten the batter into a puck shape and enclose well by stick film. Chill for in any event 30 mins, or for as long as 2 days, or freeze for a very long time.
- Then, make the filling. Put the figs, raspberries, sugar and cornflour in a large bowl and tenderly throw together, being mindful so as not to separate the raspberries, until the organic product is very much covered. Put the cardamom in a mortar and break the units with a pestle. Eliminate the seeds from their cases

and spot them back in the mortar, disposing of the units. Pound the seeds at that point add to the organic product, alongside the rosewater. Put away for 15 mins.

- Eliminate the batter from the cooler and separation into 2 pieces, one somewhat larger than the other. Re-wrap the more modest piece and put away. Separation the larger part of batter into the quantity of pies you'd prefer to make, or leave entire for a large one. On a delicately floured surface, carry out the batter to the thickness of a 50p piece, or until adequately large to line the foundation of your pie plate or tin, with a little cake overhanging. Turn the mixture over your moving pin, lift into your plate or tins, and press it well into the corners. Disperse the polenta or almonds over and spoon in the filling. Heat oven to 190C/170C fan/gas 5 and spot a preparing sheet on the center rack.
- To make a stepped plan for the highest point of the pie, carry out the cake on an all around floured sheet of preparing material . Utilize a little bread roll shaper to get rid of shapes (we've utilized a heart shaper, yet circles, jewels or blossom shapes look pretty as well). Brush the pie edge with egg, at that point slide the cake top on top. Trim the edge with scissors and press the baked good edge around the highest point of your pointer, using your thumb and the other forefinger. Work your way along the baked good edge to give an expertly fluted finish. Once covered, whisk the saved egg white and brush over the baked good.

Dissipate with some additional sugar, at that point place the pie on the preparing sheet and heat for 45 mins for a large pie, 35-40 mins for medium pies or 25-30 mins for smaller than usual pies, until the cake is brilliant and fresh and the juices are percolating. Cool for 10 mins prior to presenting with cream, crème fraîche, normal yogurt or soured cream.

Formula TIPS

Embellish YOUR PIE
1. For tips, stunts and thoughts to style the top and sides of your pie, see our manual for 11 very simple approaches to enhance a pie.
2. Stay away from THE DREADED SOGGY BOTTOM
3. To ensure your pie has a fresh covering, utilize a metal or lacquer pie plate, tin or a cake tin if your pie has a baked good base. Ensure the heating sheet is hot when the pie goes in the oven. Disperse ground almonds or polenta over the base to absorb any additional juice from the organic product.
4. ADD A GLAZE
5. Whisk extra egg white from making the baked good with a fork until foamy and utilize this to coat the pie. In the event that you need the pie to have a pleasant brilliant shading, speed in a little caster sugar as well.

Conclusion

Lastly, I hope you liked all recipes in this books. It contains delicious alkaline recipes especially made with apricots and figs which are perfect for producing alkalinity. Try and enjoy

CPSIA information can be obtained
at www.ICGtesting.com
Printed in the USA
BVHW092054040621
608822BV00004B/1079

9 781802 003345